The Top 10 Guide to Paris

By
Françoise Chaniac Dumazy

The Internationalist
96 Walter Street/Suite 200
Boston, MA 02131 US

The Internationalist®
International Business, Investment, and Travel

Published by:
The Internationalist Publishing Company
96 Walter Street/Suite 200
Boston MA 02131, USA
Tel: 617-354-7722
www.internationalist.com
PN@internationalist.com

Copyright © 1999- 2015 by PWN

The Internationalist is a Registered Trademark.
The Top 10 Guide to Paris, The Top 10 Travel Guides, The Top 10 Guide are Trademarks of the Internationalist Publishing Company

All rights are reserved under International, Pan-American, and Pan-Asian Conventions. No part of this book may be reproduced in any form without the written permission of the publisher. All rights vigorously enforced.

Code: 03112015

Titles Featured in the Top 10 Guides Series

TOP 10 GUIDE TO BEIJING

TOP 10 GUIDE TO LONDON

TOP 10 GUIDE TO LOS ANGELES

TOP 10 GUIDE TO NEW YORK CITY

TOP 10 GUIDE TO PARIS

TOP 10 GUIDE TO RIO DE JANEIRO

TOP 10 GUIDE TO ROME

TOP 10 GUIDE TO KEY FRENCH PHRASES

TOP 10 GUIDE TO KEY ITALIAN PHRASES

TOP 10 GUIDE TO KEY PORTUGUESE PHRASES

Welcome to Paris.

Paris has been the inspiration of artists, writers and lovers for centuries and the sought after prize of Emperors, Generals and Kings. What a disappointment it would be to visit Paris and not experience the very best the city has to offer.

THE TOP TEN GUIDE TO PARIS is designed so you will experience the very best of Paris: the best restaurants, the best museums, the best sights and the best entertainment. THE TOP TEN GUIDE TO PARIS is the only guide you will need. Turn the pages as a knowledgeable Parisian guides you through the best of classic and contemporary Paris.

Parisian Françoise Chaniac Dumazy makes sure you experience the city's crown jewels: the great museums, the dramatic panoramas, the romantic restaurants, the hot discos, and the classic Parisian cafes.

Whether you are visiting for a few days or a few weeks, THE TOP TEN GUIDE TO PARIS lets you focus on the best of everything so that your Paris experience is a rich and rewarding one.

Best wishes for a pleasant visit to Paris.

Françoise Chaniac Dumazy

Parisian Françoise Chaniac Dumazy knows Paris intimately and brings the city to life for readers in this dynamic guide. From her student days at the Ecole Supérieure de Commerce de Paris, in the heart of Paris, to her days as an analyst of international finance at JP Morgan, located at place Vendome, the luxury center of Paris, Françoise has recorded the best and most exciting of all that Paris has to offer. No one knows Paris like Françoise. Françoise knows the small cafés, the grand restaurants, the romantic rendezvous and the exciting discos. Françoise cuts through the clutter and delivers to you the very best of Paris so that your visit to Paris is the very best experience.

Contents

The Top Ten Things to Know When Planning your Trip

The Top Ten Things to Know for Getting Around Paris

The Top Ten Must See Areas

The Top Ten Things to Do If you want to Discover Parisians and Escape Tourists

The Top Ten Walks During the Day

The Top Ten Romantic Spots in Paris

The Top Ten Modern Architectural Sites

The Top Ten Museums

The Top Ten Small Museums

The Top Ten Art Galleries

The Top Ten Places Related to French History

The Top Ten Gardens to See

The Top Ten Bridges

The Top Ten Fountains

The Top Ten Covered Arcades

The Top Ten Squares

The Top Ten Panoramas

The Top Ten Churches

The Top Ten Things To Do with Children

The Top Ten Premium Hotels

The Top Ten Hotels (Medium Priced)

The Top Ten Budget Hotels

The Top Ten Things to Know About French Restaurants

The Top Ten Gourmet and Specialty Food Shops

The Top Ten Open-air Food Markets

The Top Ten Food Specialties

The Top Ten French Red Wines

The Top Ten French White Wines

The Top Ten French Champagnes

The Top Ten French Beers

The Top Ten Books about Paris

The Top Ten Songs about Paris

The Top Ten Movies about Paris

The Top Ten Trips outside Paris

The Top Ten Most Important Phrases You Must Know

Ten Phrases if You Don't Understand French

The Top Ten Phrases for Meeting People

The Top Ten Most Important Signs You Will See

The Top Ten Emergency Phrases

The Top Ten Medical Phrases

The Top Ten Telephone Phrases

The Top Ten Celebration Phrases

The Top Ten Gracious Phrases

The Top Ten Numbers

The Top Ten Time Terms

The Top Ten Days

The Top Ten Months (plus two)

The Top Ten Direction Phrases

The Top Ten Reference Points

The Top Ten Types of Stores

The Top Ten Shopping Phrases

The Top Ten Colors

The Top Ten Fruits

The Top Ten Vegetables

The Top Ten Train Travel Phrases

The Top Ten Airline Travel Phrases

The Top Ten Auto Terms

The Top Ten Hotel Phrases

The Top Ten Restaurant Phrases

The Top Ten Things on a Menu

The Top Ten Wine Phrases

The Top Ten Beverages

The Top Ten Things to Know When Planning your Trip

1. You need a passport (USA, Canada, and Australia citizens).

2. You do not need a visa, unless you intend to stay longer than 90 days in a row.

3. You don't need special shots.

4. Traveling by plane:
   Major airlines flying to Paris:
   • From US: American, Delta, United, and Air France
   • From Canada: Air Canada, Canadian Airlines
   • From the UK: British Airways, Air France, Virgin Atlantic, and British Midlands.Airlines fly to two airports: Orly, South of Paris; Roissy-Charles de Gaulle, North of Paris.

5. Via the Channel tunnel from the UK
   Eurostar: http://www.eurostar.com/us-en
   High speed train linking Paris and London in three hours.

6. By Ferry from the UK
   Hoverspeed: http://www.ferrytravel.com/hoverspeed-hover-speed.htm

7. Climate
   If you have the choice, the best months are certainly May, June, and September. Most Parisians leave the city in August for their annual vacations.

8. Electricity
   France runs on 220V and outlets are different. You need to buy a converter, which costs about $20, as well as an

adapter for French outlets. Adapters and converters can be found at the BHV department store, 52 rue de Rivoli, Paris 4th - métro: Hôtel de Ville.

9. Paris Tourist Office
127 av. des Champs-Elysées, Paris 8th - métro: Charles de Gaulle-Etoile
http://en.parisinfo.com/
Open daily from 9 am to 8 pm. Closed May 1.
Useful number for reserving hotels, sightseeing tours or for information on Paris. Be aware that during high season hotels are often full in Paris. Reservations are highly recommended.

10. Embassies
    - **United States**
      2 avenue Gabriel, Paris 8th - métro: Concorde
      Open weekdays from 9 am to 4 pm.
    - **Canada**
      35 av Montagne, Paris 8th - métro: Franklin D. Roosevelt
      Open weekdays from 8.30 am to 11 am.
    - **Australia**
      4 rue Jean-Rey, Paris 15th - métro: bir-Hakeim
      Open weekdays from 9 am to 5.00 pm.
    - **United Kingdom**
      35 rue du Faubourg-St-Honoré, Paris 8th - métro: Madeleine
      Open weekdays from 9.30 am to 1 pm and 2.30 pm to 6pm.

The Top Ten Things to Know for Getting Around Paris

1. To and From Roissy airport
   By bus (departure every 15 minutes): Air France buses (stop at Porte Maillot, not far from the Arc de Triomphe) or Roissy Bus (stop at Opéra).
   By train: use the RER line B

2. To and From Orly airport:
   There are several ways to get to Paris center from Orly airport By bus (departure every 15 minutes): Air France buses (stop at Invalides) or Orlybus (stop at Denfert-Rochereau).
   By train: take the Orlyval shuttle to Antony station, then the RER line B.
   By Taxi.

3. Métro
   The Métro is the ideal way to get around Paris: 15 lines cover the city and nearby suburbs. Very regular and fast trains take you anywhere in minutes. Wherever you are in Paris you'll find a metro station at less than 5-minute walking distance.

4. Buses
   Buses offer you a great view of the city. Some of the lines hit Paris' major sights:
   The bus No. 29, with its open back, goes from Gare St Lazare to the Bastille, going through Opéra, Pompidou and the Marais.
   The bus No. 72 follows the Seine, from Hôtel de Ville to Trocadéro.
   The bus No. 73 goes down the Champs-Elysées.

5. Taxis
   There are about 14,900 taxis in Paris. Nevertheless, it is sometimes difficult to find one during peak time or late at night. Taxis with lit signs are not available. The two major companies are Taxi Bleus (call 3609) and Taxi G7 (call 3607).

6. Driving in Paris
   If you plan to stay only in Paris, do not take a car. Driving in Paris can easily become a nightmare, and parking will be even worse! If you plan to rent a car (it can be useful if you want to go outside the city), you should bring along an International Driving Permit (IDP). And be aware that the legal blood alcohol level for drivers is 0.5%, the equivalent of two glasses of wine. Most major car-rental companies are represented in France at the airport or in the center of Paris:
   Avis:
   http://www.avis.com/car-rental/location/EUR/FR/Paris
   Budget:
   http://locations.budget.com/fr/paris/cdg.html
   Hertz:
   https://www.hertz.com/rentacar/car-rental/france

7. Telephones
   - Local Pay Phones
   If you want to make local telephone calls, you need to buy a calling card "50 or 120 calling units" at a tobacco shop, metro station or post office. Calling cards only.
   - International Calls
   To phone abroad from France, dial 00+country code+local code+phone number. To call France from abroad, dial the international code+33+region code (1 for Paris skip the zero)+8-digit number.
   - Cellular Phones
   European cellular operators use a different technology than in North America. Thus, if you want or need to stay in touch while in Paris or anywhere in Europe, you will need to rent a GSM-900 phone from a specialized company in Europe.

8. Arrondissements
   Paris is divided up into 20 districts, called "arrondissements". The first eight arrondissements are the most central and contain most of the best sights. The last two digits of the zip code give the arrondissement (75011 is the eleventh arrondissement for instance).

9. River: left bank / right bank
   When talking about a place or giving an address, the Parisians often refer to the right bank (rive droite) and the left bank (rive gauche) of the Seine. The "rive gauche" is the artistic and student area, including the Quartier Latin and St-Gemain-des- Prés, while the "rive droite" is more traditional and commercial; on that side you'll find the Marais, the Louvre, the Opéra neighborhoods and the Champs-Elysées.

10. French Floor Numbering System
   The French floor system is different from the American one: in France the first floor corresponds to the second floor in the U.S.
   • Street level (US) Floor zero or "rez-de-chaussée"
   • 2nd floor (US) 1st Floor - "premier étage"
   • 3rd floor (US) 2nd floor - "deuxieme etage"
   • Basement (US) Basement - "sous-sol"

The Top Ten Must See Areas

There are some "classics" in Paris that you simply cannot miss if you want to discover the French capital.

1. Le Louvre
   34-36 quai du Louvre, Paris 1st - métro: Palais Royal
   http://www.louvre.fr/en
   Monday, Thursday, Saturday, Sunday from 9 am to 6 pm, and Wednesday and Friday 9 am-9.45pm. Closed on Tuesdays.
   Former home of the French kings, the Louvre is now the largest museum in the world. It has been recently renovated, enlarged and embellished. You'll find magnificent collections of Oriental, Egyptian, Greek, Etruscan and Roman antiquities, French sculptures, objets d'art, French paintings and the paintings of the Northern Schools (including Rubens). Don't miss the most famous masterpieces: the Venus de Milo, the Victory of Samothrace and the Mona Lisa by Leonardo da Vinci.

2. Place des Vosges – Marais
   Paris 4th - métro: Saint-Paul or Chemin-Vert
   Inaugurated in 1612 as Place Royale, the Place des Vosges is the most elegant square in Paris, with its stylish red and white brick residences, its arcades and its lovely garden. It is located in the heart of the Marais, the oldest district in Paris, where you'll find splendid private mansions.

3. Notre-Dame
   6 place du Parvis de Notre-Dame, Paris 4th - métro: Cité or St- Michel
   Open weekdays from 9.30 am to 6 pm, weekends from 9 am to 6 pm.
   Built between 1163 and 1345, Notre-Dame cathedral is a masterpiece of French Gothic art. It is located on the Ile

de la Cité, where the Parisii first settled in the third century before Jesus Christ.

4. Ile Saint-Louis
   Paris 4th - métro: Pont-Marie
   The small Ile Saint-Louis is one of the most charming and romantic spots in Paris.

5. Quartier Latin
   Paris 5th & 6th - métro: Saint-Michel, Odéon, Maubert-Mutualité, Jussieu or Cardinal-Lemoine
   The Latin Quarter has a large population of students and academics. Among the prestigious institutions of higher education, you'll find the Sorbonne, the Collège de France, and the Ecole Normale Supérieure. This district has become more and more touristy over the past few years. Don't miss the lively Mouffetard street and the Contrescarpe square, the shop-lined boulevard St-Michel, and the romantic Jardin du Luxembourg.

6. Champs Elysées
   Paris 8th - métro: Franklin D. Roosevelt or George V or Charles de Gaulle-Etoile
   The world's most famous avenue has become very touristy. You still have a great perspective with the Louvre and place de la Concorde in the bottom and the Arche de la Défense behind the Arc de Triomphe.

7. Musée d'Orsay
   1 rue de Bellechasse, Paris 7th - métro: Solférino or Rue du Bac
   http://www.musee-orsay.fr/en/home.html
   Open daily from 10 am to 6 pm (9.15 pm on Thursdays). Closed on Mondays. During the summer the museum opens at 9 am.
   The Orsay train station, inaugurated for the World Exhibition of 1900, was transformed into a museum devoted to the art of the second half of the 19th century.

8. Eiffel Tower
   Champ de Mars, Paris 7th - métro: Bir-Hakeim, Champ de Mars – Tour Eiffel, Pont de l'Alma
   Open daily from 9.30 am to 11 pm (to midnight in July and August) While the public abhorred it upon its conception, it became the symbol of Paris and is now famous worldwide. From the top of the tower you have a great view over the capital.

9. Place Vendôme
   Paris 1st - métro: Opéra or Tuileries
   One of the most elegant squares in Paris, home to the most famous jewelry shops and to the Ritz hotel.

10. Montmartre and the Sacré-Coeur
    From the métro: Anvers, climb the Montmartre hill to reach the basilica Sacré-Coeur and then the lively Place du Tertre filled with cafés, restaurants and portrait

artists. A few blocks southwest, you'll find the famous red-light district, Pigalle, and along the boulevards de Clichy and de Rochechouart the famous cabarets and nightclubs, including the Moulin- Rouge.

The Top Ten Things to Do If you want to Discover Parisians and Escape Tourists

1. Spend a few hours in a very Parisian Café, on boulevard St-Germain.

2. Discover French food at one of the liveliest street markets on Rue Mouffetard (Paris 5th).

3. Eat ice cream at Berthillon, Paris' best ice cream shop, on Ile Saint-Louis.

4. Go window-shopping along the Faubourg St-Honoré and the Place Vendôme.

5. Have a rest in the Square du Vert-Galand, on the Ile de la Cité.

6. Around five o'clock, have a delicious pastry with tea in a very cozy "salon de thé" (tea-room) in the Marais.

7. Take a boat tour on the Seine at night.

8. Go to the ballet at Opéra Garnier.

9. Spend all your savings in one of most the famous restaurants to discover fine French cooking and flavorful wines.

10. On Sunday, go for a walk in Bois de Boulogne and discover where Parisian families spend their week-ends and get a breath of fresh air.

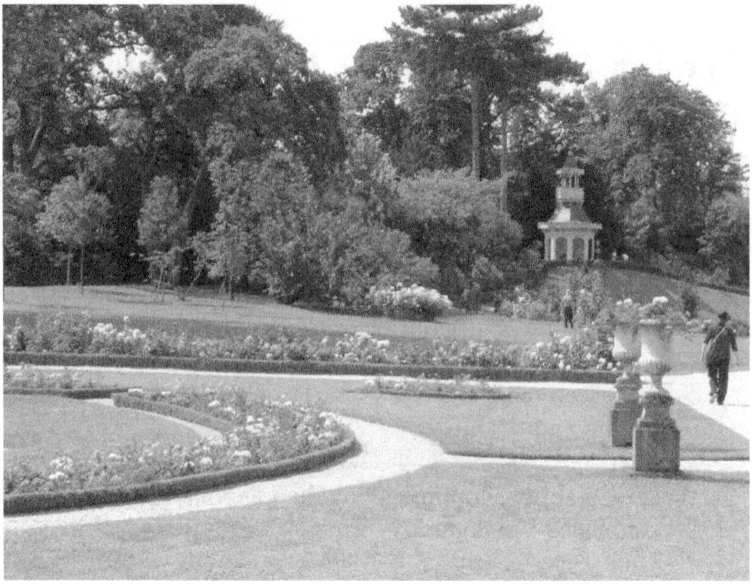

The Top Ten Walks During the Day

Paris is the ideal city for walkers: walking in Paris is never boring; every 100-meters you discover an attractive building, a charming square or an old boutique. Some neighborhoods are particularly pleasant for strollers.

1. The Marais
   The Marais is the most lively, charming and trendy neighborhood in Paris. It covers the 3rd and 4th arrondissements. Not to miss: the Jewish quarter around rue des Rosiers, the elegant place des Vosges, the gay district around the rue Vieille du Temple and rue Ste-Croix de la Bretonnerie, and the great rue des Francs-Bourgeois with its nice boutiques and restaurants.

2. Saint-Germain des Prés
   The other trendy and pleasant district in Paris, frequented by students and artists. Not to miss: the charming place Saint- Sulpice and place de Furstenberg, the boulevard St-Germain and its famous cafés (Le Flore, Les Deux Magots) and chic boutiques, the rue

Bonaparte and its art galleries, the rue Visconti and rue St-André-des-Arts.

3. Ile Saint-Louis and Ile de la Cité
Walk along the charming rue St-Louis-en-l'Ile, take the footbridge to the Ile de la Cité, and go through the small garden behind Notre-Dame. After visiting the two most beautiful churches in Paris, Notre-Dame and Sainte-Chapelle, go through the quiet place Dauphine and finally have a rest in the romantic Square du Vert-Galand.

4. Opéra, Palais Royal, Jardin des Tuileries and the Louvre
From the busy Opéra Garnier square, go down on the avenuede l'Opéra, take a left on the rue des Petits Champs (don't miss the Galerie Vivienne) until the beautiful place des Victoires, then go through the Jardins du Palais Royal and end in the newly embellished Jardins des Tuileries.

5. Quartier Latin: rue Mouffetard, Panthéon, Jardin du Luxembourg
It's a pleasure to get lost among the narrow streets in the Latin Quarter, the centre of French intellectual life. Don't miss the Sorbonne, the labyrinth streets between the Seine and place Maubert, and the rue Mouffetard and rue de la Montagne-Ste-Geneviève behind the Panthéon. Finally, if you're tired, have a rest in the romantic Jardin du Luxembourg.

6. Place Vendôme, Rue Royale, Rue du Faubourg-St-Honoré
Between the Place Vendôme, Madeleine and the Rond-Point des Champs-Elysées, there are some of the most chic streets in Paris. You'll find jewels around the place Vendôme, crystal and china on rue Royale and clothing on rue du Faubourg- St-Honoré.

7. Champs-Elysées, Avenue Montaigne
   From the Pont de l'Alma, walk on avenue Montaigne which houses the famous Haute Couture boutiques, then from Concorde, walk up on the Champs-Elysées, finally go to the top of the Arc de Triomphe from which you'll have a great view to the capital.

8. Montmartre
   The highest hill in Paris, site of the basilica Sacré-Coeur, has the atmosphere of a village. Rapidly escape from the very touristy square "du Tertre", and discover the picturesque streets: rue Junot, villa Léandre and rue des Saules, where you'll find the last remaining vineyard in Paris.

9. Champ de Mars, Tour Eiffel, Trocadéro
   A classic: after a walk through the Champ de Mars from where you can admire beautiful private houses, climb the Eiffel Tower for a nice view, then cross the river and reach the Trocadéro.

10. Centre Pompidou, Les Halles
    Don't miss the lively rue Montorgueil with its food market, the Eglise St-Eustache and the pleasant square behind the Halles, and of course the area around Centre Georges Pompidou with its street musicians and performers.

The Top Ten Romantic Spots in Paris

Is Paris the most romantic city in the world? Here are a few addresses to help you answer the question...

1. Square du Vert-Galand
   Paris 1st - métro: Pont-Neuf
   Very quiet and romantic garden at the tip of Ile de la Cité, offering a great view over the Seine.

2. Ile Saint-Louis
   Paris 4th - métro: Pont-Marie
   Very charming and romantic island in the heart of Paris.

3. Top of the Tour Eiffel at night
   Champ de Mars, Paris 7th - métro: Bir-Hakeim, Champ de Mars – Tour Eiffel, Pont de l'Alma
   Open daily from 9.30 am to 11 pm (to midnight in July and August)
   For a very romantic evening, you can have dinner in Jules Verne restaurant, which serves excellent food.

4. Place des Vosges
   Paris 4th - métro: Saint-Paul or Chemin-Vert
   During the weekend many artists play music under the arcades surrounding the square, creating a great atmosphere.

5. Jardin du Luxembourg
   Paris 6th - métro: Odéon or St-Michel or RER Luxembourg
   One of the most romantic parks in Paris.

6. Place de Furstemberg
   Paris 6th - métro: Mabillon
   A very pretty square in the heart of the Latin Quarter.

7. Place du marché Sainte-Catherine
   Paris 4th - métro: Saint-Paul
   Very intimate square in the heart of the Marais, surrounded by restaurants.

8. Jardins des Tuileries
   Paris 1st - métro: Tuileries or Concorde
   Former royal garden when the Louvre was the home of French kings, the Jardins des Tuileries have recently been embellished and are very pleasant today. Nice view

over the Louvre, place de la Concorde and Musée d'Orsay.

9. Pont des Arts
   Built in 1804 and located next to the Louvre, this footbridge is a meeting spot for artists and painters.

10. Jardins du Palais Royal
    Paris 1st - métro: Palais Royal-Musée du Louvre
    Surrounded by beautiful covered galleries, this park was the site of many historical events.

The Top Ten Modern Architectural Sites

Built in the 1980s and 1990s, the Grande Arche de la Défense, the pyramids of the Louvre, the Opéra Bastille and the very new Bibliothèque Nationale were part of President Mitterrand's "grands projets." Some of them caused controversy.

1. Centre Georges Pompidou
   19 rue Beaubourg, Paris 4th - métro: Châtelet Les Halles
   https://www.centrepompidou.fr/en
   More than 600 architects from around the world competed to work on President Pompidou's project to build a huge art center in Paris. The Italian Piano and the British Rogers were chosen finally. The very modern building, made of metal, glass and pipes was finished in 1977 and was very controversial among Parisians; some of them were horrified! Today it is one of the most visited places in Paris. It houses the National Museum of Modern Art, the Public Information Library, the Institute of Acoustic and Musical Research and the Department for Cultural Development.

2. Institut du Monde Arabe
   1 rue des Fossés Saint-Bernard, Paris 5th - métro: Jussieu, Cardinal-Lemoine or Sully-Morland
   www.imarabe.org
   Open Tuesday, Wednesday, Thursday from 10 am to 7 pm, Friday, Saturday, Sunday from 10 am to 7 pm, closed Mondays.
   Conceived by Jean Nouvel, this beautiful building contains an array of Arab-Islamic art, textiles, and ceramics.

3. La Grande Arche de la Défense
   1 parvis de la Défense, 92040 Paris la Défense - métro:,La Défense
   Officially opened in 1989, it holds special events and temporary exhibitions.

4. Opéra Bastille
   Place de la Bastille, Paris 12th - métro: Bastille
   https://www.operadeparis.fr/
   Inaugurated in 1989, this opera house is one of the most modern in the world.

5. Bibliothèque Nationale de France (National Library)
   Quai François Mauriac, Paris 13th - métro: Quai de la gare
   http://www.bnf.fr/en/tools/a.welcome_to_the_bnf.html
   Open daily from 10 am to 7 pm, Sundays from 1 pm to 7 pm. Closed on Mondays.
   Conceived by François Mitterrand, the new national library has been inaugurated in 1997: four modern buildings that look like books standing open. With its 395 km of shelves, it is one of the largest libraries in the world.

6. Pyramides du Louvre
   Conceived by the architect Peï, the striking all-in-glass pyramid now has its "sister", the reversed pyramid inside the commercial gallery of Carroussel du Louvre.

7. La Géode (Cité des Sciences et de l'Industrie)
   30 av. Corentin Cariou, Paris 19th - métro: Porte de la Villette
   https://www.lageode.fr/?lang=en
   Open daily from 10:30 am to 8:30 pm. Closed on Mondays.
   The Geode is a modern cinema with hemispheric screen.

8. Parc André Citroën
   Paris 15th - métro: Balard
   Futuristic park with varied gardens, waterfalls, sculptures.

9. Tour Montparnasse 56
   33 av. du Maine, Paris 15th - métro: Montparnasse-Bienvenüe
   http://www.tourmontparnasse56.com/en/#/home
   The tallest office building (210 meters / 690 feet) from which one has a great view.

10. Les colonnes du Buren (Palais Royal)
    Paris 1st - métro: Palais-Royal
    These striped columns inside the park of the Palais Royal may disappoint you. When constructed, they were the subject of great debate among Parisians.

The Top Ten Museums

If you plan to visit many museums and monuments, you can buy the "Carte Musées et Monuments", a card which gives you free entry to 65 important venues in Paris. The cost for 1/3/5 days is 70/140/200 francs. It is available from the venues or tourist offices.

1. Musée du Louvre
   34-36 quai du Louvre, Paris 1st - métro: Palais Royal
   Ph: 01.40.20.53.
   Monday, Thursday, Saturday, Sunday from 9 am to 6 pm; Wednesday and Friday from 9 am to 9.45 pm. Closed on Tuesdays.
   Former home of the French kings, the Louvre is now the largest museum in the world. It has been recently renovated, enlarged and embellished. You'll find magnificent collections of Oriental, Egyptian, Greek, Etruscan and Roman antiquities, French sculptures, objets d'art, French paintings and the paintings of the Northern Schools (including Rubens). Don't miss the most famous masterpieces: the Venus de Milo, the Victory of Samothrace and the Mona Lisa by Leonardo da Vinci.

2. Musée d'Orsay
   1 rue de Bellechasse, Paris 7th - métro: Solférino or Rue du Bac
   http://www.musee-orsay.fr/en/home.html
   Open daily from 9.30 am to 6 pm (9.15 pm on Thursdays). Closed on Mondays. During the summer the museum opens at 9 am.
   The Orsay train station, inaugurated for the World Exhibition of 1900, was transformed into a museum devoted to the artistic creation of the second half of the 19th century. Masterpieces by Van Gogh (L'Eglise d'Auvers-sur-Oise), Monet (Nymphéas bleus), Renoir and Cézanne.

3. Musée National d'Art Moderne - Centre Georges Pompidou
   19 rue Beaubourg, Paris 4th - métro: Châtelet Les Halles
   http://www.mam.paris.fr/en
   The National Museum of Modern Art houses famous paintings by Kandinsky, Delaunay, Klee, Miro, Dali, among many others.

4. Musée Picasso
   Hôtel de Juigné – Salé 5 rue de Thorigny, Paris 3rd - métro: Saint-Paul or Chemin-Vert
   http://www.museepicassoparis.fr/en/
   Open weekdays from 11.30 am to 6 pm, weekends from 9.30 am to 6 pm. Closed on Monday.
   In the heart of the Marais, exceptional collection of Picasso's paintings and sculptures.

5. Musée Rodin
   Hôtel Biron 77 rue de Varenne, Paris 7th - métro: Varenne
   http://www.musee-rodin.fr/en
   Open daily from 10 am to 5.45 pm (8.45 pm on Wednesdays). Closed on Mondays.
   One of the most beautiful museums in Paris which houses all the most famous works by the sculptor Auguste Rodin.

6. Cité des Sciences et de l'Industrie La Villette
   30 av. Corentin Cariou, Paris 19th - métro: Porte de la Villette
   http://www.cite-sciences.fr/en/home/
   Open daily from 10 am to 6 pm (7 pm on Sundays). Closed on Mondays.
   This center presents the great technological achievements.
   • Explora: permanent exhibitions on the earth and the universe, languages and communication, technological and industrial developments.
   • The Planetarium.
   • The children's city and the techno city: play areas and interactive areas for children.
   • The Geode: cinema with hemispheric screen (every hour from 10 am to 9 pm).
   • Cinaxe: an earth-shaking experience (every 15 minutes from 11 am to 6 pm).

7. Grand Palais
   3 av. du Général Eisenhower, Paris 8th - métro: Champs-Elysées-Clémenceau or Franklin-Roosevelt
   http://www.grandpalais.fr/visite/en/
   Open daily from 10 am to 8 pm (10 pm on Wednesdays). Closed on Tuesdays.
   Prestigious temporary exhibitions.

8. Musée Carnavalet
   23 rue de Sévigné, Paris 3rd - métro: Saint-Paul
   http://www.carnavalet.paris.fr/
   Open daily from 10 am to 6 pm. Closed on Mondays.
   Located in two beautiful private mansions in the Marais, this museum describes the history of Paris through splendid collections.

9. Musée National d'Histoire Naturelle
   57 rue Cuvier, Paris 5th - métro: Jussieu or Gare d'Austerlitz
   http://www.mnhn.fr/fr/visitez/galeries-jardins-zoos
   Consult the website for hours of specific museums within the Musée National d'Histoire Naturelle, such as the Jardin des Plantes.
   Don't miss the "Grande Galerie de l'Evolution", with impressive zoological collections.

10. Institut du Monde Arabe
    1 rue des Fossés Saint-Bernard, Paris 5th - métro: Jussieu, Cardinal-Lemoine or Sully-Morland
    http://www.imarabe.org/
    Open Tuesday, Wednesday, Thursday from 10 am to 6 pm, Friday to 9.30 pm, weekends to 7 pm. Closed on Mondays.
    The Institute of the Arab World contains a beautiful array of Arab-Islamic art, textiles, and ceramics from the 7th to the 19th century. Restaurant and terrace on the 9th floor with a great view over Paris.

The Top Ten Small Museums

Paris houses numerous small museums dedicated to one artist or one type of art. Some of them are outstanding.

1. Musée Marmottan Claude Monet
   2 rue Louis-Boilly, Paris 16th - métro: La Muette
   http://www.marmottan.fr
   Open from Tuesday to Sunday from 10 am to 6 pm, 9 pm on Thursday. Masterpieces by Claude Monet and other Impressionist paintings (Gauguin, Renoir, Sisley).

2. Musée de l'Orangerie
   Jardin des Tuileries, Paris 1st - métro: Concorde
   http://www.musee-orangerie.fr/
   Open daily from 9 am to 6 pm. Closed on Tuesdays.
   Houses the famous Nymphéas by Claude Monet.

3. Musée Jacquemart-André
   158 blvd Haussmann, Paris 8th - métro: Miromesnil
   http://musee-jacquemart-andre.com/en/home
   Open daily from 10 am to 6 pm.
   Exceptional art collection of Edouard André and Nélie Jacquemart in their private mansion (Italian renaissance and 18th century French paintings). Very pleasant restaurant.

4. Musée de l'Armée - Hôtel des Invalides
   129 Rue de Grenelle, Paris 7th - métro: Latour Maubourg or Varenne
   http://www.musee-armee.fr/en/english-version.html
   Open daily from 10 am to 6 pm (5 pm from October to March).
   Houses a collection of weapons and uniforms of the French army. The Eglise du Dôme houses the tomb of Napoléon 1st.

5. Espace Dali Montmartre
   1 rue Poulbot, Paris 18th - métro: Abbesses or Lamarck-Caulaincourt
   http://daliparis.com/
   Open daily from 10 am to 6 pm, 8 pm in July and August. Exhibition of the works of the Spanish surrealist artist Salvador Dali.

6. Musée National du Moyen-Age, Thermes de Cluny
   6 place Paul-Painlevé, Paris 5th - métro: Cluny, Saint-Michel or Odéon
   http://www.musee-moyenage.fr/
   Open daily from 9.15 am to 5.45 pm. Closed on Tuesdays. Medieval art.

7. Musée National Eugène Delacroix
   6 rue de Furstemberg, Paris 6th - métro: Saint-Germain-des-Prés, Mabillon
   http://www.musee-delacroix.fr/en/
   Open daily from 9.30 am to 12 pm and 1.30 pm to 5 pm. Closed on Tuesdays.
   Paintings and personal items of Delacroix in his studio on Furstemberg square.

8. Musée de la Mode et du Textile
   Palais du louvre 107 rue de Rivoli, Paris 1st - métro: Palais-Royal
   http://www.musee-delacroix.fr/en/
   Open Tuesday to Sunday from 11 am to 6 pm (until 9 pm on Thursdays)
   Exceptional collection of costumes from the 17th to the 20th century.

9. Musée de la Marine
   Palais de Chaillot
   Place du Trocadéro, Paris 16th - métro: Trocadéro
   www.musee-marine.fr
   Open daily fron 11 am to 6 pm, 7 pm on weekends. Closed on Tuesdays.
   Maritime history from the 18th century to today.

10. Musée National Gustave Moreau
    14 rue de la Rochefoucault, Paris 9th - métro: Trinité
    www.musee-moreau.fr
    Open daily from 10 am to 12.45 pm and 2 pm to 5.15 pm, Mondays and Wednesdays from 11 am to 5.15 pm. Closed on Tuesdays.

The Top Ten Art Galleries

The avenue Matignon (right bank) and the rue des Beaux Arts (left bank) are the two main locations for art galleries.

1. Galerie Claude Bernard
   5-7 rue des Beaux-Arts, Paris 6th - métro: St-Germain-des-Prés
   http://www.claude-bernard.com/index.php
   Open from Tuesday to Saturday, from 9:30 am to 12:30 pm and from 2:30 pm to 6:30 pm.
   Splendid gallery with works by Bacon, Monnard, Botero, Giacometti.

2. Galerie Lelong
   13 rue de Téhéran, Paris 8th - métro: Franklin D. Rossevelt
   www.galerie-lelong.com/fr
   Open from Tuesday to Frida, 10:30 am to 6 pm, Saturdays from 2 pm to 6:30 pm.
   One of the most important galleries in Paris. Works by great 20th century artists: Giacometti, Miró, Alechinsky, James Brown, and Stenberg.

3. Modus Art Gallery
   23 Place des Vosges, Paris 3rd – métro: Chemin Vert
   www.modusartgallery.com
   Open daily from 10:30 am to 8 pm.
   Display of contemporary and modern art in the Marais district.

4. Galerie Schmit
   396 rue St-Honoré, Paris 1st - métro: Concorde
   http://www.galerieschmit.com/
   Open daily from 9 am to 12.30 pm and 2 pm to 6.30 pm.
   Closed Saturdays, Sundays.
   Works by great artists of the 19th and 20th century: Delacroix, Chagall, Dufy, Utrillo and many others.

5. Galerie Xippas
   108 rue Vieille du Temple, Paris, Paris 3rd – métro: Saint-Sébastien-Froissart or Filles du Calvaire
   www.xippas.net
   Open Tuesday to Friday from 10 am to 1 pm, 2 pm to 7 pm, Saturdays from 10 am to 7 pm.
   Focused on international contemporary art, a platform for discovery and promotion of both young and established artists.

6. Millesime Gallery
   41 avenue de la Bourdonnais, Paris 7th – métro: Ecole Militaire or Pont de l'Alma.
   www.millesime-gallery.com
   Open daily from 10 am to 7 pm. Closed Sundays.
   A photography gallery close to the Eiffel Tower.

7. Bernheim Jeune
   83 rue du Faubourg St-Honoré, Paris 8th - métro: Champs-Elysées-Clémenceau
   www.bernheim-jeune.com/
   Open daily from 10.30 am to 12.30 pm and 2.30 pm to 6.30 pm.
   Closed Sundays, Mondays.
   Works by Monet and Pissaro.

8. Didier Imbert Fine Arts
   19 av. Matignon, Paris 8th - métro: Miromesnil
   Ph: +33.1.42.25.86.03
   Open daily from 10 am to 1 pm and 2.30 pm to 7 pm.
   Closed Sundays.
   Works by Botero, Wesselmann, Brauner, Brancusi.

9. Bugada & Cargnel
   7-9 rue de l'Equerre, Paris 19th - métro: Pyrénées
   www.bugadacargnel.com
   Open Tuesday to Saturday from 2 pm to 7 pm, and by appointment.
   Works from French and international emerging artists.

10. Galerie Laurent Godin
    5 rue du Grenier St Lazare, Paris 3rd – métro: Rambuteau
    www.laurentgodin.com/gallery.html
    Open Tuesday to Saturday from 11 am to 7 pm.
    Three main show rooms with contemporary photography, paintings, and sculpture.

The Top Ten Places Related to French History

Many buildings and squares in Paris were the scene of the capital's historic events.

1. Place de la Concorde
   Métro: Concorde
   Execution of Louis XVI and Marie-Antoinette in 1793 during the Reign of Terror.

2. Place de la Bastille
   Métro: Bastille
   The Bastille prison was stormed by a Parisian mob on 14 July 1789: it was the beginning of the French Revolution. The Reign of Terror followed.

3. Hôtel des Invalides - Musée de l'armée (military museum)
   Esplanade des Invalides, Paris 7th - métro: Latour-Maubourg or Varenne
   www.musee-armee.fr/

Open daily from 10 am to 6 pm (5 pm from November to March).
The Hôtel des Invalides was commissioned by Louis XIV to house wounded soldiers. Napoléon's tomb is housed in the Eglise du Dôme.

4. La Conciergerie
   Blvd du Palais, quai de l'Horloge - métro: Cité
   conciergerie.monuments-nationaux.fr
   April-Sept: open daily from 9.30 am to 6 pm; Oct-March: open daily from 10 am to 4.30 pm.
   A magnificent example of the architecture of the 14th century, the Conciergerie was the prison where Marie-Antoinette was kept during the French Revolution.

5. Le Louvre
   34-36 quai du Louvre, Paris 1st - métro: Palais-Royal
   www.louvre.fr
   Former home of the French kings until Louis XIV decided to move to Versailles.

6. Place des Vosges
   Métro: Saint-Paul or Chemin-Vert
   Inaugurated in 1612 as the royal square.

7. Palais Royal
   Métro: Palais-Royal
   Housed young king Louis 14th in the 1640s.

8. L'Arc de Triomphe de l'Etoile
   Paris 8th - métro: Charles de Gaulle – Etoile
   This colossal Triumphal Arch was planned by Napoléon to celebrate his successes.

9. Panthéon
   Place du Panthéon, Paris 5th - métro: Cardinal-Lemoine, Maubert-Mutualité or RER Luxembourg
   Open from 9.30 am to 6.30 pm (10 am to 5.30 pm from October to March)

Since the French Revolution, the Panthéon has housed the ashes of the "great citizens of France", including Voltaire, Rousseau, Victor Hugo, Jean Moulin, André Malraux.

10. Musée Carnavalet
    23 rue de Sévigné, Paris 3rd - métro: St-Paul
    www.carnavalet.paris.fr
    Open daily from 10 am to 6 pm. Closed on Mondays.
    Located in two beautiful private mansions in the Marais, this museum describes the history of Paris through splendid collections.

The Top Ten Gardens to See

There are many small gardens and parks inside the capital. But if you really need a breath of fresh air, you'd better go to the Bois de Boulogne or Bois de Vincennes at the periphery of Paris.

1. Jardin du Luxembourg
   Paris 6th - métro: Odéon or St-Michel or RER Luxembourg
   One of the most romantic parks in Paris.

2. Jardins des Tuileries
   Paris 1st - métro: Tuileries or Concorde
   Former royal garden when the Louvre was French kings' home, the Jardins des Tuileries have just been embellished and are very pleasant today. Nice view over the Louvre, place de la Concorde and Musée d'Orsay.

3. Bois de Boulogne
   Paris 16th - métro: Porte Maillot, Porte Dauphine or Porte d'Auteuil.
   With 35 km of footpaths, 8 km of cyclepaths and 29 km of bridleways, the Bois de Boulogne is the largest park in Paris. After boating on Lac Inférieur, don't miss the fantastic flower collection of the Parc de Bagatelle.

4. Jardin du Palais Royal
   Paris 1st - métro: Palais Royal-Musée du Louvre
   Surrounded by beautiful covered galeries, this park was the site of many historical events.

5. Parc Montsouris
   Paris 14th - RER Cité Universitaire or métro: Porte d'Orléans
   Charming garden with its artificial lake, caves and waterfalls.

6. Parc des Buttes Chaumont
   Paris 19th - métro: Buttes-Chaumont
   Bordered by rues de Crimée, Manin and Botzaris, Paris 19th - métro: Buttes-Chaumon.
   Nice lake overlooked by a promontory.

7. Parc Monceau
   Paris 17th - métro: Monceau
   In the heart of one of the most elegant residential districts.

8. Jardin des Plantes
   Paris 5th - métro: Jussieu, Monge or Gare d'Austerlitz
   Houses over 10,000 varieties of plants.

9. Jardin du Champ-de-Mars
   Paris 7th - métro: Ecole Militaire or RER Champ-de-Mars
   Designed to enhance the Eiffel Tower. Large lawns open to the public.

10. Bois de Vincennes
    Paris 12th - métro: Chateau de Vincennes, Porte Dorée, Porte de Charenton or Liberté
    Another very large park in the southeast of Paris. Houses a zoo.

The Top Ten Bridges

Paris without its bridges would not be Paris! All the important architectural sites are situated around the Seine and its 36 bridges.

1. Pont-Neuf
   The oldest (built in the 16th century) and the most famous bridge in Paris. Very present in the French movie "Les Amants du Pont-Neuf."

2. Pont Alexandre III
   Inaugurated for the World Exhibition of 1900, this heavy bridge with angels and gold horses is the most extravagant bridge in Paris.

3. Pont des Arts
   Built in 1804 and located next to the Louvre, this footbridge is a meeting spot for artists and painters.

4. Pont de l'Archeveché
   Beautiful view over the cathedral Notre-Dame.

5. Pont Saint-Louis
   Footbridge linking the two islands Ile de la Cité and Ile Saint-Louis.

6. Pont Bir-Hakeim
   Beautiful view over the Eiffel Tower.

7. Pont de la Concorde
   Splendid view over the Place de la Concorde.

8. Pont Mirabeau
   Immortalized by the French poet Apollinaire.

9. Pont Royal
   One of the oldest bridges in Paris, along with Pont-Neuf.

10. Pont de la Tournelle
    Pleasant view over Notre-Dame and Ile St-Louis.

The Top Ten Fountains

At one time, Paris had over 20,000 thousands fountains. Here are the most dramatic ones still remaining:

1. Fontaine Stravinsky
   Place Igor Stravinsky (beside the Centre Pompidou) Paris 4th - métro: Les Halles.
   Fanciful and colorful fountains created by Jean Tinguely and Niki de Saint-Phalle.

2. Fontaine des Innocents
   Square des Innocents, Paris 1st - métro: Châtelet-Les Halles.
   Designed by Pierre Lescot and sculptured by Jean Goujon, it's a chef-d'oeuvre of the Renaissance period.

3. Fontaine de la Croix-du-Trahoir
   Rue St-Honoré & Rue de l'Arbre Sec, Paris 1st - métro: Louvre- Rivoli

4. Fontaine de la Place de la Concorde
   Place de la Concorde, Paris 8th - métro: Concorde

5. Fontaine de l'Observatoire
   Avenue de l'Observatoire - RER Port-Royal or métro: Vavin
   Famous for the four parts of the world sculptured by Carpeaux.

6. Fontaine Saint-Michel
   Place St-Michel, Paris 6th - métro: St-Michel

7. Fontaine de Médicis - Jardin du Luxembourg
   Jardin du Luxembourg - RER Luxembourg or métro: St-Michel

8. Fontaine des Quatre Evèques
   Place St-Sulpice, Paris 6th - métro: Saint-Sulpice

9. Fontaine Molière
   Rue Richelieu & rue Molière, Paris 1st - métro: Palais-Royal Visconti built this foutain near the house where Molière died.

10. Fontaine du Châtelet
    Place du Châtelet, Paris 1st - métro: Châtelet

The Top Ten Covered Arcades
"Passages couverts"

Built at the beginning of the 19th century, these iron-and-glass covered arcades, which housed shops, restaurants, and theatres, were part of the social life. While many were demolished or fell into disrepair during the 20th century, some of them have been rescued and refurbished.

1. Galerie Véro-Dodat (1826)
   19 rue Jean-Jacques Rousseau, Paris 2nd - métro: Palais-Royal
   The most beautiful gallery with very nice boutiques.

2. Galerie Vivienne (1823)
   4 rue des Petits-Champs, Paris 2nd - métro: Bourse
   Built in 1823, it is today one of the most lively galleries.

3. Passage Choiseul (1827)
   23 rue des Augustins, Paris 2nd - métro: Quatre-Septembre
   The writer Louis-Ferdinand Céline lived there when he was a child; he gives a dark description of it in "Mort à credit."

4. Passage des Panoramas (1800)
   11 blvd Montmartre, Paris 2nd - métro: Rue-Montmartre
   First "passage couvert" in Paris, described by Zola in his novel "Nana."

5. Galerie Colbert (1826)
   6 rue Vivienne, Paris 2nd - métro: Bourse

6. Passage Jouffroy (1845)
   10 blvd Montmartre, Paris 2nd - métro: Rue-Montmartre
   First heated gallery in Paris.

7. Passage Verdeau (1847)
   6 rue de la Grange-Bateliere, Paris 9nd - métro: Richelieu-Drouot or Le Pelletier.
   You'll find antiques and old books.

8. Passage du Grand-Cerf (1825)
   145 rue Saint-Denis, Paris 4th - métro: Etienne Marcel

9. Passage Brady
   18 rue du Faubourg-Saint-Denis, Paris 9th - métro: Strasbourg-Saint-Denis.

10. Passage du Caire
    Rue du Caire, Paris 2nd - métro: Réaumur-Sebastopol or Sentier

The Top Ten Squares

Each Parisian district has its own square and each square has its own story...

1. Place des Vosges
   Paris 4th - métro: Saint-Paul or Chemin-Vert
   The most elegant square in Paris with its red and white brick residences and its stylish garden. Inaugurated in 1612 as the royal square.

2. Place Vendôme
   Paris 1st - métro: Opéra or Tuileries
   Built during the reign of Louis XIV, this magnificent square now hosts the most famous jewelry shops and the Ritz hotel, Europe's most somptuous hotel.

3. Place de la Concorde
   Paris 8th - métro: Concorde
   Beautiful square where many important historic events occurred, including the execution of Louis XVI. A 3,300 year-old Egyptian obelisk stands at its center.

4. Place de la Bastille
   Paris 12th - métro: Bastille
   Site of the 1789 revolution.

5. Place des Victoires
   Paris 2nd - Métro: Palais-Royal or Bourse
   Superb square with its matching facades designed in 1685 by Versailles architect Hardouin-Mansart. Now home to many fashion boutiques.

6. Place Dauphine
   Paris 1st - métro: Pont-Neuf
   A very charming and quiet square which used to be an important royal square.

7. Place du Marché Sainte-Catherine
   Paris 4th - métro: Saint-Paul.
   Very intimate square in the heart of the Marais, surrounded by restaurants.

8. Place de Furstemberg
   Paris 6th - métro: Mabillon
   A very pretty square in the heart of the Latin Quarter.

9. Place du Tertre
   Paris 18th - métro: Anvers or Abesses
   The main square of the village of Montmartre, filled with cafés, restaurants and portrait artists.

10. Place du Palais-Royal
    Paris 1st - métro: Palais-Royal
    Borders on the Royal Palace gardens and the Comédie Française.

The Top Ten Panoramas

Many rooftops of Paris offer beautiful views over the city and its monuments both day and night.

1. Tour Eiffel
   Champ de Mars, Paris 7th - métro: Bir-Hakeim
   www.toureiffel.paris
   Open daily from 9:30 am to 11 pm (to midnight in July and August).
   Spectacular view from the top of Paris' most famous monument. You can take the lift or the stairs up to the 2nd level and another lift takes you up to the 3rd level (top).

2. Tour Montparnasse
   33 av. du Maine, Paris 15th - métro: Montparnasse
   www.tourmontparnasse56.com
   Great view from Paris' tallest office building (210 meters /
   690 feet).

3. Towers of Notre-Dame
   Place du Parvis Notre-Dame, Paris 4th - métro: Cité
   notre-dame-de-paris.monuments-nationaux.fr
   Open daily from 10 am to 6.30 pm (5:30 pm from mid-October to March).
   Exceptional view of the heart of Paris.

4. Dôme du Sacré Coeur
   35 rue du Chevalier-de-la-Barre, Paris 18th - métro: Anvers
   www.sacre-coeur-montmartre.com
   Open daily from 8:30 am to 8 pm (9 am to 5 pm from October to April).
   Panoramic view over the capital from the top of the basilica. From the parvis of the Basilica, you also have a great view on Parisian monuments.

5. Arc de Triomphe
   Place Charles de Gaulle-Etoile - métro: Charles de Gaulle-Etoile
   arc-de-triomphe.monuments-nationaux.fr
   Open daily from 10 am to 11 pm (Apr-Sept), from 10 am to 10.30 pm (Oct-Mar).
   Great view over the Champs-Elysées.

6. Centre Georges-Pompidou (5th floor terrace)
   Métro: Les Halles
   Open daily from 11 am to 9 pm, closed on Tuesdays.

7. Parc de Belleville
   47 rue des Couronnes, Paris 11th – métro: Pyrénées
   The park opens at 8 am during the week, 9 on weekends. Closing time depends on season.
   Situated on the top of a hill and a wonderful off-the-beaten-track destination.

8. Le Printemps
   64 blvd Haussmann, Paris 9th - métro: Havre-Caumartin

www.printemps.com/magasins/paris-haussman
Open daily from 9.35 am to 8 pm (8:45 pm on Thursdays). Closed on Sundays.
From the terrace of the department store, there is a great view over the Opéra Garnier, Montmartre and Madeleine church.

9. Institut du Monde Arabe (9th floor terrace)
1 rue des Fossés Saint-Bernard, Paris 5th - métro: Jussieu, Cardinal-Lemoine or Sully-Morland
www.imarabe.org
Open Tuesday, Wednesday, Thursday from 10 am to 7 pm, Friday, Saturday, Sunday from 10 am to 7 pm, closed Mondays.
Panoramic view over Notre-Dame, Ile Saint-Louis and Ile de la Cité.

10. La Grande Arche de la Défense
1 Parvis de la Défense, Puteaux, France
Métro: La Défense
www.grandearche.com
Open daily from 10 am to 8 pm.
Beautiful view over La Défense area.

The Top Ten Churches

1. Notre-Dame de Paris
   6 place du Parvis de Notre-Dame, Paris 4th - métro: Cité or St Michel
   www.notredamedeparis.fr
   Open daily from 8 am to 6:45 pm (7:15 pm on weekends).
   Built between 1163 and 1345, Notre-Dame cathedral is a masterpiece of French Gothic art.

2. La Sainte Chapelle
   4 blvd du Palais, Paris 1st - métro: Cité
   sainte-chapelle.monuments-nationaux.fr
   Open daily from 9:30 am to 6:30 pm from March to October, 9 am to 5 pm from November to February.
   Located within the Paris law courts, Sainte-Chapelle is a pearl of gothic art. Many concerts take place here.

3. Basilique du Sacré-Coeur
   Place St-Pierre, Paris 18th - métro: Anvers
   www.sacre-coeur-montmartre.com
   Open daily from 6 am to 10:30 pm.
   This byzantine style basilica is Montmartre's best known monument.

4. Saint-Etienne-du-Mont
   1 rue St-Etienne-du-Mont, Paris 5th - métro: Cardinal-Lemoine
   www.saintetiennedumont.fr
   Open on Tuesdays to Fridays from 8:45 am to 7:45 pm, Saturdays from 8:45 am to noon and 2 pm to 7:45 pm, Sundays from 8:45 am to 12:15 pm and 2 pm to 7:45 pm. Closed on Mondays, July and August.
   Lovely church which houses the remains of Sainte-Geneviève, the patron saint of Paris. Don't miss its graceful rood screen and its carved wooden pulpit.

5. Basilique Saint-Denis
   Place de l'Hôtel-de-ville, St-Denis - métro: St-Denis-Basilique
   saint-denis.monuments-nationaux.fr
   Open from 10 am to 6:15 pm (Sundays open at 12 pm)from April to September, 10 am to 5 pm (Sundays open at 12 pm) from October to March.
   The burial place for many French kings, including Catherine de Médicis, Marie Antoinette and Louis XIV.

6. La Madeleine
   Place de la Madeleine, Paris 8th - métro: Madeleine
   www.eglise-lamadeleine.com
   Open daily from 9:30 am to 7 pm.
   At the request of Napoleon 1st, it was built as a replica of a greco-roman temple.

7. Saint-Eustache
   2 rue du Jour, Paris 1st - métro: Les Halles
   www.saint-eustache.org
   Open weekdays on Monday to Friday from 9:30 am to 7 pm, Saturday from 10 am to 7 pm, Sunday from 9 am to 7 pm.
   Nice example of Gothic art.

8. Saint-Germain-des-Prés
   Place St-Germain-des-Prés, Paris 6th métro: St-Germain-des Prés
   www.eglise-sgp.org
   The oldest Roman church in Paris.

9. Saint-Séverin
   1 rue des Prêtres St-Séverin, Paris 5th - métro: St-Michel
   www.saint-severin.com
   Free concerts often performed on Sundays.

10. Saint-Sulpice
    Place St-Sulpice, Paris 6th - métro: St-Sulpice
    pss75.fr/saint-sulpice-paris/
    Half-hour organ concerts on Sundays at 11.30 am.

The Top Ten Things To Do with Children

1. La Cité des Enfants
   Cité des Sciences et de l'Industrie, Parc de la Villette
   30 av Corentin-Cariou, Paris 19th - métro: Porte de la Villette
   www.cite-cite-sciences.fr/fr/au-programme/expos-permanentes/la-cite-des-enfants/
   A part of the Cité des Sciences et de l'Industrie is specially dedicated to children. 90-minute "discovery" programs are held every day. Fun experiments to discover the human body, the weather, the world of animals...

2. Musée National d'Histoire Naturelle
   (Museum of Natural History)
   Jardin des Plantes
   36 rue Geoffroy St-Hilaire, Paris 5th - métro: Gare d'Austerlitz or Censier-Daubenton
   www.mnhn.fr
   Don't miss the newly renovated "Grande Galerie de l'Evolution", with impressive zoological collections.

3. Eurodisney
   Marne-la-Vallée-Chessy (RER line A4)
   www.disneylandparis.fr
   The only Disneyland in Europe, with two parks.

4. Bois de Boulogne, Jardin d'Acclimatation
   Paris 16th - métro: Sablons, Porte Maillot, la Muette or Porte d'Auteuil
   www.jardindacclimatation.fr
   A very nice place for the whole family to go canoeing, sunbathe or have a picnic in summer. There is also an amusement park for kids.

5. Jardin des Tuileries
   Paris 1st - métro: Tuileries or Concorde
   Pony rides, toy sailboats and puppet shows.

6. Parc Astérix
   30km north of Paris
   www.parcasterix.fr
   Come and discover Astérix and Obélix, the heroes of the most famous French comic strip.

7. Palais de la Découverte
   Av. Franklin D. Roosevelt, Paris 8th - métro Franklin-Roosevelt
   www.palais-decouverte.fr
   The ancestor of the Cité des Sciences et de l'Industrie. Although a little old-fashioned, it's still very interesting.

8. Musée Grévin
   10 blvd Montmartre, Paris 9th - métro: Rue-Montmartre
   www.grevin-paris.com
   A wax museum with famous figures, from François Mitterrand to Claudia Schiffer.

9. Parc zoologique de Paris
   Route de la ceinture du Lac, Paris 12th - métro: Porte-Dorée or Château-de-Vincennes
   www.parczoologiquedeparis.fr

10. Jardin du Luxembourg
    Paris 6th - métro: Cluny-la-Sorbonne or RER Luxembourg
    Pony rides, toy sailboats and puppet shows.

The Top Ten Premium Hotels

Paris has some of the most elegant hotels in the world. They are pricey but worth the experience if you can afford it.

1. Hôtel Ritz
   15 place Vendôme, Paris 1st - métro: Opéra
   www.ritzparis.com
   One of the most luxurious hotels in the world.

2. Hôtel de Crillon
   10 place de la Concorde, Paris 8th - métro: Concorde
   www.crillon.com
   On Concorde square, a 200-year-old building which used to be the palace of the Duc de Crillon.
   Currently closed for renovation; check www.rosewoodhotels.com for more details

3. Plaza Athénée
   25 av. Montaigne, Paris 8th - métro: Franklin D. Roosevelt
   www.dorchestercollection.com/en/paris/hotel-plaza-athenee

4. George V Four Seasons
   31 av. George V, Paris 8th - métro: George V
   www.fourseasons.com/paris

5. Hôtel Meurice
   228 rue de Rivoli, Paris 1st - métro: Tuileries or Concorde
   www.dorchestercollection.com/en/paris/le-meurice

6. Hotel Le Bristol
   112 rue du Faubourg St-Honore, Paris, 75008
   www.lebristolparis.com/eng/welcome

A palace with opulent décor, attentive staff who speak English, and a key location parallel to the Champ-Elysees.

7. Mon Hotel Paris
   1-5 rue d'Argentine, Paris, 75116
   www.monhotel.fr
   A boutique, five-star home away from home.

8. Lutetia
   45 blvd Raspail, Paris 6th - métro: Sèvres-Babylone
   Currently closed for renovation until 2017.

9. Royal Monceau
   37 av. Hoche, Paris 8th - métro: Hoche
   www.leroyalmonceau.com

10. Radisson Blu Le Dokhan's Hotel
    117 rue Lauriston, Paris, 75116
    www.radissonblu.com/dokhanhotel-paristrocadero

The Top Ten Hotels (Medium Priced)

Paris also has many affordable hotels with a lot of charm and class. Expect double rooms around $200.

1. Hôtel des Marronniers
   21 rue Jacob, Paris 6th - métro: St-Germain-des-Prés
   www.hoteldesmarronniers.com
   A lot of charm. Breakfast served daily in a lovely small garden.

2. Hotel Verneuil
   8 rue de Berneuli, Paris, Paris 7th – métro: Rue du Bac
   www.hotel-verneuil-saint-germain.com
   A hotel full of romance and sophistication.

3. Hotel Seven
   20 rue Berthollet, Paris 5th - métro: Les Gobelins
   www.sevenhotelparis.com
   A hotel with futuristic décor hiding behind a traditional, Parisian façade.

4. The Five Hotel
   3 rue Flatters, Paris 5th - métro: Les Gobelins
   www.thefivehotel.com
   This hotel could double as a modern art exhibit.

5. Hotel de Varenne
   44 rue de Bourgogne, Paris 7th - métro: Varenne
   www.varenne-hotel-paris.com
   A simple hotel with French charrm.

6. La Villa St. Germain
   29 rue Jacob, Paris 6th - métro: Saint-Germain-des-Prés
   www.hotelvillasaintgermain.com
   A modern hotel just steps from the Louvre.

7. Minerve Hotel
   13 rue des Ecoles, Paris 5th - métro: Cardinal Lemoine
   www.parishotelminerve.com
   A traditional hotel in the heart of Paris's Latin Quarter that offers private parking.

8. Castex Hotel
   5 rue Castex, Paris 4th - métro: Bastille
   www.castexhotel.com
   A 17th-century style hotel located on the border between the Bastille sector and the Marais.

9. New Orient Hotel
   16 rue de Constantinople, Paris 8th - métro: Europe or Villiers
   www.hotelneworient.com
   A small, well-kept hotel in the 8th district. Perfect for those looking for a more residential experience.

10. Hotel Relais Bosquet Paris
    19 rue du Champ de Mars, Paris 7th - métro: Ecole Militaire
    www.hotel-paris-bosquet.com
    A hotel right by the Eiffel Tower. Offers three breakfast packages!

The Top Ten Budget Hotels

1. Hôtel de l'Espérance
   15 rue Pascal, Paris 5th - métro: Censier-Daubenton
   www.hoteldelesperance.fr
   Elegant rooms, professional staff.

2. Familia Hôtel
   11 rue des Ecoles, Paris 5th - métro: Jussieu or Maubert Mutualité or Cardinal-Lemoine
   www.hotel-paris-familia.com
   Attractive and friendly; nice view from the 5th and 6th floors.

3. Grand Hôtel Léveque
   29 rue Cler, Paris 7th - métro: Ecole Militaire or Latour-Maubourg
   www.hotel-leveque.com
   Very close to the Eiffel tower with updated amenities.

4. Hôtel Vivienne
   40 rue Vivienne, Paris 2nd - métro: Rue-Montmartre or Richelieu-Drouot or Bourse
   www.hotel-vivienne.com

5. Hôtel Emile
   2 rue Malher, Paris 4th - métro: St-Paul
   www.hotelemile.com

6. Hotel Apollon Montparnasse
   91 rue de l'Ouest 14 Arr., Paris 14th - métro: Pernety
   www.paris-hotel-paris.net
   This hotel's convenient location and nice neighborhood make up for its small rooms.

7. Hotel Moderne Saint Germain
   33 rue des Ecoles, Paris 5th - métro: Mutualité
   www.hotel-paris-stgermain.com
   Under a ten-minute walk to Paris's main attractions, this hotel, located in the Latin Quarter, has a modern décor with complementary Wi-Fi and air-conditioned rooms.

8. Lux Hotel Picpus
   74 boulevard de Picpus, Paris 12th - métro: Picpus
   www.lux-hote-picpus.com
   A cheap but comfortable hotel in a quiet area near a metro hub.

9. Hotel des Grandes Ecoles
   75 rue de Cardinal- Lemoine, Paris 5th - métro: Cardinal Lemoine
   www.hotel-grandes-ecoles.com
   A pastoral little cottage located near the Contrescarpe.

10. Hotel des Arts Bastille
    2 rue Godefroy Cavaignac Paris 11th - métro: Charonne
    www.paris-hotel-desarts.com
    This hotel is located in the Bastille Opera and renovated its rooms in 2011.

The Top Ten Things to Know About French Restaurants

Paris is one of the world's greatest food capitals. Here are a few things you should know before going to a French restaurant.

1. "Menu" versus "à la carte"
   Restaurants generally serve a three-course meal at lunch and dinner. This fixed-price meal is called the "menu." If you don't choose this formula, you take "à la carte." It is always much cheaper to take the fixed-price "menu."

2. Wines
   "Cru" suggests a wine of superior quality. A "grand cru" or "premier cru" should be even more superior wine. Wine in "carafe" or "pichet" is usually ordinary table wine.

3. Water
   A "carafe d'eau" means tap water while "eau minérale" means a bottle of mineral water, "gazeuse" for carbonated or "plate" for not.

4. Service and tax included ("service compris")
   The prices that figure on the menu include service and tax.

5. Tipping
   Although the service is already included in the price, you can leave a tip for a very friendly waiter.

6. Lunch and dinner time
   Lunch is served between noon and 2 pm or 2.30 pm. Dinner is served between 7 pm and 10 pm or 11 pm. Some restaurants serve all night.

7. Fromage ou Dessert
   After the main course, you can choose cheese or dessert, or both. Most fixed-price menus include "cheese or dessert" or "cheese and dessert."

8. Espresso
   Another very French habit: take an espresso at the end of the meal. Be aware that if you ask for a "coffee," you won't get a large cup of coffee, but a small espresso!

9. Bistro versus Brasserie
   Bistros and Brasseries are both very Parisian institutions. The bistro is a kind of wine bar which serves simple and traditional home-style cooking. The brasserie is the French version of the pubs: single course dishes served with a beer.

10. Smoking / Non-smoking
    Although it is a legal requirement to have two separate rooms, smoking and non-smoking, you'll notice that many restaurants, especially the small bistros and cafés, do not really respect the law.

The Top Ten Gourmet and Specialty Food Shops

1. Berthillon
   31 rue Saint-Louis-en-l'Ile, Paris 4th - métro: Pont-Marie
   www.berthillon.fr
   The best ice cream in Paris.

2. Fauchon
   26 place de la Madeleine, Paris 8th - métro: Madeleine
   www.fauchon.com
   Luxury delicatessen.

3. Hédiard
   21 place de la Madeleine, Paris 8th - métro: Madeleine
   www.hediard.com
   Luxury delicatessen. A large variety of spices.

4. La Durée
   75, avenue des Champs Elysées, Paris 8th - métro: Georges V, Charles de Gaulle Etoile
   World-renowned macarons with numerous signature flavors.

5. La Grande Epicerie
   38 rue de Sèvres, Paris 7th - métro: Sèvre-Babylone
   www.lagrandeepicerie.com

6. Debauve & Gallais
   30 rue des Saints-Pères, Paris 6th - métro: St-Germain-des-Prés
   www.debauveandgallais.com
   Also 107, rue Jouffroy d'Abbans, 17th (métro: Charles de Gaulle-Etoile) and 33, rue de Vivienne, 2nd (métro: Bourse)
   Heaven on earth for chocolate lovers!

7. Lenôtre
   48 av. Victor Hugo, Paris 16th - métro: Victor Hugo
   www.lenotre.com
   Famous French caterer Gaston Lenôtre has several boutiques in Paris.

8. Au Verger de la Madeleine
   4 blvd Malesherbes, Paris 8th - métro: Madeleine
   Vintage wine merchant with an outstanding selection of wines and spirits.

9. Dalloyau
   101 rue du Faubourg-S-Honoré, Paris 8th - métro: St-Philippe-du-Roule
   www.dalloyau.fr
   Very good pastries.

10. Poilâne
    8 rue du Cherche-Midi, Paris 6th - métro: St-Sulpice
    www.poilane.fr
    Lionel Poilâne makes the most famous bread in the world.

The Top Ten Open-air Food Markets

Go off the beaten path and experience one of the numerous open-air food markets in Paris.

1. Rue Mouffetard
   Paris 5th - métro: Censier-Daubenton
   A lively and picturesque place.

2. Rue Montorgueil
   Paris 2nd - métro: Les Halles
   A bustling street with old food shops.

3. Place d'Alligre
   Paris 12th - métro: Ledru-Rollin
   The cheapest and most dynamic market in Paris.

4. Place Monge
   Paris 5th - métro: Place Monge

5. Rue de Lévis
   Paris 17th - métro: Villiers
   Pleasant pedestrian street with a picturesque market.

6. Boulevard Richard-Lenoir
   Paris 11th - métro: Bastille or Richard-Lenoir

7. Rue de Busi and Rue de Seine
   Paris 6th - métro: Odéon

8. Rue Cler
   Paris 7th - métro: Ecole Militaire

9. Rue de Passy
   Paris 16th - métro: Passy

10. Avenue de Saxe
    Paris 7th - métro: Duroc

The Top Ten Food Specialties

French cooking may be very different from a region to another. Here are the most typical French dishes, that you will eat nowhere else.

1. Blanquette de Veau
   Veal cooked in white sauce, served with rice.

2. Boeuf Bourguignon
   Beef cooked in red wine (from Burgundy).

3. Cassoulet
   Sausage and chicken with beans (from Toulouse).

4. Foie gras
   Very fine appetizer made of pure duck or goose liver (from the Southwest of France).

5. Coq au vin
   Chicken in red wine.

6. Pot au feu
   Beef and vegetable hotpot.

7. Choucroute
   Variety of sausages served with sauerkraut (from Alsace).

8. Cuisses de grenouille
   Frogs legs cooked with garlic, parsley, and butter.

9. Bouillabaisse
   Marseille specialty consisting of a variety of fishes cooked together.

10. Escargots
    Snails cooked with parsley and butter.

The Top Ten French Red Wines

French red wines are produced in different regions, of which the most famous are: Bordeaux (in the Southwest), Bourgogne (Burgundy), Loire valley, and Rhône valley.

1. Médoc 1er cru (Bordeaux)

2. Vosne Romanée (Bourgogne - Côtes de Nuits)

3. Pomerol (Bordeaux)

4. Pommard (Bourgogne - Côtes de Beaune)

5. Saint Emilion (Bordeaux)

6. Saint Julien (Bordeaux)

7. Châteauneuf du Pape (Côtes du Rhône)

8. Aloxe Corton (Bourgogne - Côtes de Beaune)

9. Nuits Saint Georges (Bourgogne - Côtes de Nuits)

10. Saint-Joseph (Côtes du Rhône)

The Top Ten French White Wines

Like red wines, white wines are produced in different regions.

1. Sauterne (Bordeaux)

2. Pouilly-Fuissé (Bourgogne)

3. Condrieu (Côtes du Rhône)

4. Gewurtzraminer (Alsace)

5. Sancerre Blanc (Loire)

6. Pouilly-Fumé (Loire Valley)

7. Jurançon (Southwest of France)

8. Château Chalon (Jura)

9. Riesling (Alsace)

10. Graves Blanc (Bordeaux)

The Top Ten French Champagnes

Most champagnes are produced in Reims area, at about 150km east of Paris.

1. Dom Pérignon
2. Deutz
3. Moët & Chandon
4. Roderer
5. Ruinart
6. Veuve Cliquot
7. Mum
8. Taittinger
9. Piper-Heidsieck
10. Lanson

The Top Ten French Beers

Although France is not the best place for beer, French beer is drunk in large quantities in the country.

1. Kronenbourg
2. Kanterbrau
3. Stella Artois
4. 1664
5. Jeanlain
6. Pelforth
7. Jupiler
8. Killian's
9. Adelscott
10. La Bière du Démon

The Top Ten Books about Paris

1. Notre-Dame de Paris - Victor Hugo
2. Au Bonheur des Dames - Emile Zola
3. Mémoires d'une jeune fille rangée - Simone de Beauvoir
4. Bel Ami - Guy de Maupassant
5. Le Père Goriot - Honoré de Balzac
6. Le ventre de Paris - Emile Zola
7. Paris - Julien Green
8. La Place de l'Etoile - Patrick Modiano
9. Nocturne Parisien - Paul Verlaine
10. La Fée Carabine - Daniel Pennac

The Top Ten Songs about Paris

1. Il est cinq heures, Paris s'éveille - Jacques Dutronc
2. Le poinçonneur des lilas - Serge Gainsbourg
3. Les Champs-Elysées - Joe Dassin
4. Sous le ciel de Paris - Edith Piaf
5. Les prénoms de Paris - Jacques Brel
6. Pont Mirabeau - Léo Ferré
7. Paris Canaille - Juliette Gréco
8. Comme ils disent - Charles Aznavour
9. Le bateau-mouche - Alain Souchon
10. Revoir Paris - Charles Trénet

The Top Ten Movies about Paris

1. Hôtel du Nord (1938) - Marcel Carné

2. Le Dernier Métro (1980) - François Truffaut

3. Chacun Cherche son Chat (1996) - Cédric Klapisch

4. Les Enfants du Paradis (1955) - Marcel Carné

5. Last Tango in Paris (1972) - Bernardo Bertolluci

6. La Passante du Sans Souci (1981) - Jacques Rouffio

7. A Bout de Souffle (1959) - Jean-Luc Godard

8. Les 400 Coups (1959) - François Truffaut

9. Subway (1985) - Luc Besson

10. Un Monde Sans Pitié (1989) - Eric Rochant

The Top Ten Trips outside Paris

1. Versailles
   Visitor information at 7 rue des Réservoirs
   en.chateauversailles.fr
   Closed on Mondays.
   The "Château de Versailles" housed several generations of French royalty. Its history began when Louis XIV transformed his father's hunting lodge into a palace of unimaginable opulence. Don't miss the splendid Hall of Mirrors (where the famous Treaty of Versailles was signed), the king's chambers and the queen's apartments, and the beautiful gardens with their elaborate fountains.

2. The Gardens of Giverny
   80km northwest from Paris.
   giverny.org/gardens/jardins.htm
   From 1883 to 1926, the impressionist Claude Monet painted his most famous works in the gardens of Giverny.

3. Château de Chantilly
   Chantilly 45km north of Paris.
   www.chantilly-tourisme.com
   Mon-Wed 10am - 6pm, Nov-Feb 10.30am - 12.45pm/ 2pm- 5pm
   Beautiful gardens and many superb paintings.
   Musée Vivant du Cheval (Living Horse Museum)
   Wed-Mon 10.30 am - 5.30 pm.
   Don't miss the magnificent "Grandes Ecuries" (stables) next to Chantilly's famous "Champ de course" (racecourse).

4. Cathédrale Notre-Dame de Chartres
   Tourist office at 16 Cloitre Notre-Dame.
   www.cathedrale-chartres.org
   Open daily from 7.30 am to 7 pm.
   A 50 minute ride by train from Gare Montparnasse
   Magnificent gothic cathedral built in the 13th century.

5. Château de Vaux-le-Vicomte
   77950 Maincy
   www.vaux-le-vicomte.com
   Don't miss the candlelight evenings every Saturday from 8.30pm to 11 pm (from May to mid-October).

6. Château et Forêt de Fontainebleau
   Visitor information at 31 place Napoléon-Bonaparte
   www.musee-chateau-fontainebleau.fr

7. Saint-Germain-en-Laye
   Office de Tourisme: 38 rue au Pain
   www.saintgermainenlaye.fr
   Access: RER Line A1
   St-Germain-en-Laye is a wealthy Parisian suburb that looks like a provincial town. Its castle was transformed by Napoleon III into a museum of antiquity: Musée des Antiquités Nationales.

8. Loire Valley
   The Loire Valley, in the middle of French countryside, is known as the playground of the Kings. Among the most beautiful châteaux: the large and gorgeous Château Chambord, the lovely renaissance Azay-le-Rideau, and the Château de Chenonceau, an architectural wonder straddling the river Cher.

9. Mont-Saint-Michel
   Office de Tourisme de la Baie du Mont St-Michel 3bis grande rue des Stuarts 35120 Dol-de-Bretagne
   www.ot-montsaintmichel.com
   A great natural site.

10. The D-Day landing beaches in Normandy
    250km northwest of Paris.
    Comité Régional de Tourisme de Normandie
    14 rue Charles Corbeau 72000 Evreux
    www.normandie-tourisme.fr
    e-mail: info@normandy-tourism.org
    A very interesting trip to immerse oneself in World War II history. Do not miss the impressive American cemetery overlooking Omaha Beach, the Pointe-du-Hoc, Ste-Mère Eglise, and the history museum at Arromanches.

The Top Ten Most Important Phrases You Must Know

1. Yes
   Oui

2. No
   Non

3. Hello / Good morning/ Good afternoon
   Bonjour

4. Goodbye
   Au revoir

5. Please
   S'il vous plaît

6. Thank you
   Merci

7. You're welcome
   Je vous en prie

8. Excuse me
   Excusez-moi

9. Sorry
   Désolé / Pardon

10. Where is...?
    Où est...?

Ten Phrases if You Don't Understand French

1. Please excuse my poor French.
   Veuillez excuser mon mauvais français.

2. Do you speak English?
   Parlez-vous anglais?

3. I can't speak French.
   Je ne parle pas français.

4. I don't understand.
   Je ne comprends pas.

5. How do you say... in French?
   Comment dit-on... en français?

6. Could you please spell it?
   Est-ce que vous pouvez l'épeler?

7. Could you please write that down?
   Est-ce que vous pouvez l'écrire?

8. Could you please repeat slowly?
   Est-ce que vous pouvez répéter lentement?

9. Could you please translate this?
   Est-ce que vous pouvez me traduire ceci?

10. Do you have a dictionary English-French?
    Avez-vous un dictionnaire anglais-français?

The Top Ten Phrases for Meeting People

1. My name is...
   Je m'appelle...

2. What is your name?
   Comment vous appelez-vous? (formal)
   Comment t'appelles-tu? (informal)

3. Pleased to meet you
   Enchanté(e) / Très heureux (se).

4. How are you?
   Comment allez-vous?
   Comment vas-tu?

5. Where are you from?
   D'où venez-vous?
   D' où viens-tu?

6. I'm from...
   Je viens de...

7. Do you live in Paris?
   Est-ce que vous habitez à Paris?
   Est-ce que tu habites à Paris?

8. Could we get together while I am here?
   Pourrions-nous nous voir pendant que je suis ici?

9. My telephone number is ...
   Mon numéro de téléphone est le ...

10. I will call you.
    Je vous appellerai / je t'appellerai

The Top Ten Most Important Signs You Will See

1. Ladies
   Dames

2. Gentlemen
   Messieurs

3. Elevator
   Ascenseur

4. Stairs
   Escaliers

5. Push
   Poussez

6. Pull
   Tirez

7. Exit
   Sortie

8. Emergency exit
   Sortie de secours

9. Do not enter
   Interdit

10. No smoking
    Interdit de fumer

The Top Ten Emergency Phrases

1. Help!
   A l'aide!
   Au secours!

2. I need help.
   J'ai besoin d'aide.

3. It's an emergency!
   C'est une urgence!

4. Call the Police.
   Appelez la police.

5. Get me the Police.
   Allez me chercher la police.

6. It hurts.
   J'ai mal.

7. I need to get to a hospital.
   Je dois aller à l'hôpital.

8. I need a doctor.
   Il me faut un médecin.

9. I need an ambulance.
   Il me faut une ambulance.

10. I have been attacked.
    J'ai été attaqué(e).

The Top Ten Medical Phrases

1. I feel very sick.
   Je me sens très malade.

2. Please get me a doctor.
   Appelez-moi un docteur s'il vous plaît.

3. Do you have any aspirins?
   Avez-vous de l'aspirine?

4. I have a temperature.
   J'ai de la température.

5. I am allergic to...
   Je suis allergique à...

6. My stomach is upset.
   J'ai mal à l'estomac.

7. I have a headache.
   J'ai mal à la tête.

8. Should I go to a hospital?
   Est-ce que je dois aller à l'hôpital?

9. How do I get to a hospital?
   Comment est-ce que je vais à l'hôpital?

10. Where is the nearest pharmacy?
    Où se trouve la pharmacie la plus proche?

The Top Ten Telephone Phrases

1. Hello
   Allo

2. Who is calling?
   De la part de qui?

3. Hold on.
   Ne quittez pas.

4. Just a minute.
   Un instant.

5. May I speak to...?
   Pourrais-je parler à...?

6. He / She is on the line.
   Il / Elle est en ligne.

7. Do you want to wait?
   Voulez-vous patienter?

8. I do not speak French. Do you speak English?
   Je ne parle pas français. Parlez-vous anglais?

9. Can I leave him/her a message?
   Est-ce que je peux lui laisser un message?

10. I will call back later.
    Je rappellerai plus tard.

The Top Ten Celebration Phrases

1. Cheers!
   A votre santé!

2. Happy Birthday!
   Joyeux Anniversaire!

3. Congratulations!
   Félicitations!

4. Great!
   Super!

5. Wonderful!
   Formidable!

6. Merry Christmas!
   Joyeux Noël!

7. Happy New Year!
   Bonne Année!

8. Happy holidays!
   Bonnes vacances!

9. Good luck!
   Bonne chance!

10. Excellent!
    Excellent!

The Top Ten Gracious Phrases

1. Thank you.
   Merci.

2. Thanks a lot.
   Merci beaucoup.

3. Thank you so much.
   Merci infiniment.

4. It is so kind of you.
   C'est très gentil de votre part.

5. Thank you for your hospitality.
   Merci pour votre hospitalité.

6. Thank you for your help.
   Merci pour votre aide.

7. I'd like to thank you.
   Je vous remercie.

8. Thanks a lot for the wonderful meal.
   Merci beaucoup pour ce délicieux repas.

9. You have a lovely family.
   Vous avez / tu as une famille formidable.

10. You look very nice.
    Vous êtes / tu es resplendissant(e).

The Top Ten Numbers

1. One
   Un

2. Two
   Deux

3. Three
   Trois

4. Four
   Quatre

5. Five
   Cinq

6. Six
   Six

7. Seven
   Sept

8. Eight
   Huit

9. Nine
   Neuf

10. Ten
    Dix

The Top Ten Time Terms

When speaking, French people use both the 24-hour time system and the a.m./p.m. system. All time schedules are on the 24-hour system.

1. What time is it?
   Quelle heure est-il?

2. It is two a.m.
   Il est deux heures du matin.

3. It is two p.m.
   Il est quatorze heures / Il est deux heures de l'après-midi.

4. It is half past three.
   Il est trois heures et demie. / Il est quinze heures trente.

5. It is noon / midnight.
   Il est midi / minuit.

6. In the morning / in the afternoon
   Le matin / l'après-midi

7. This morning / This afternoon/ Tonight
   Ce matin / Cet après-midi / Ce soir

8. At what time do you close / open?
   A quelle heure est-ce que vous fermez / ouvrez?

9. I will be there at ...
   Je serai là à ...

10. I am sorry for being late.
    Je suis désolé(e) d'être en retard.

The Top Ten Days

1. Monday
   Lundi

2. Tuesday
   Mardi

3. Wednesday
   Mercredi

4. Thursday
   Jeudi

5. Friday
   Vendredi

6. Saturday
   Samedi

7. Sunday
   Dimanche

8. Today
   Aujourd'hui

9. Tomorrow
   Demain

10. This weekend
    Ce week-end

The Top Ten Months (plus two)

1. January
   Janvier

2. February
   Février

3. March
   Mars

4. April
   Avril

5. May
   Mai

6. June
   Juin

7. July
   Juillet

8. August
   Août

9. September
   Septembre

10. October
    Octobre

11. November
    Novembre

12. December
    Décembre

The Top Ten Direction Phrases

1. On the right
A droite

2. On the Left
A gauche

3. Straight ahead
Tout droit

4. Turn
Tournez

5. Is it far from here?
C'est loin d'ici?

6. Is it within walking distance?
Peut-on y aller à pied?

7. Where is the nearest subway station?
Où se trouve la station de métro la plus proche?

8. I am looking for ...
Je cherche ...

9. Could you tell me where is ...
Pouvez-vous m'indiquer où se trouve ...

10. What is the shortest way to go ... ?
Quel est le chemin le plus court pour aller ... ?

The Top Ten Reference Points

1. Avenue
   Avenue

2. Boulevard
   Boulevard

3. Street
   Rue

4. North / South
   Nord / Sud

5. West / East
   Ouest / Est

6. City center
   Centre ville

7. In the suburbs
   Dans la banlieue

8. I am at...
   Je suis à ...

9. Where is ...
   Où est ..

10. Square
    Place

The Top Ten Types of Stores

1. Pharmacy
   Pharmacie

2. Food store
   Magasin d'alimentation / Epicerie

3. Department store
   Grand magasin

4. Men's clothing store
   Magasin de vêtements pour hommes

5. Women's clothing store
   Magasin de vêtements pour femmes

6. Bookstore
   Librairie

7. Bakery
   Boulangerie

8. Pastries shop
   Pâtisserie

9. Flower store
   Fleuriste

10. Caterer
    Traiteur

The Top Ten Shopping Phrases

1. How much?
   Combien?

2. It's too expensive.
   C'est trop cher.

3. Do you have anything less expensive?
   Avez-vous quelque chose de moins cher?

4. Do you have anything about 100 francs?
   Avez-vous quelque chose dans les 100 francs?

5. Do you have it in other colors?
   Est-ce que vous l'avez dans d'autres couleurs?

6. Do you have it in my size?
   Est-ce que vous l'avez dans ma taille?

7. Would you please giftwrap it?
   Pouvez-vous faire un paquet cadeau s'il vous plaît?

8. Do you take credit cards?
   Est-ce que vous acceptez les cartes de crédit?

9. Do you take traveler checks?
   Est-ce que vous acceptez les chèques de voyage?

10. I need a receipt please.
    J'ai besoin d'un reçu s'il vous plaît.

The Top Ten Colors

1. Black
   Noir

2. White
   Blanc

3. Blue
   Bleu

4. Green
   Vert

5. Red
   Rouge

6. Yellow
   Jaune

7. Pink
   Rose

8. Brown
   Marron

9. Orange
   Orange

10. Beige
    Beige

The Top Ten Fruits

1. Apple
   Pomme

2. Orange
   Orange

3. Strawberries
   Fraises

4. Grapes
   Raisin

5. Pineapple
   Ananas

6. Pear
   Poire

7. Cherries
   Cerises

8. Peach
   Pêche

9. Banana
   Banane

10. Raspberries
    Framboises

The Top Ten Vegetables

1. Potatoes
   Pommes de terre

2. Green beans
   Haricots verts

3. Tomatoes
   Tomates

4. Eggplants
   Aubergines

5. Zucchini
   Courgettes

6. Lettuce
   Laitue

7. Mushrooms
   Champignons

8. Green peas
   Petits pois

9. Asparagus
   Asperges

10. Spinach
    Epinards

The Top Ten Train Travel Phrases

1. I'd like a one-way / return ticket
   Je voudrais un billet aller simple / aller retour

2. Do I need to change trains?
   Est-ce que je dois changer de train?

3. What time does the next train leave?
   A quelle heure part le prochain train?

4. First / second class
   Première / seconde classe

5. Platform
   Le quai

6. Ticket
   Le billet

7. Smoking / Non smoking
   Fumeur / Non fumeur

8. Which track is it on? "Track 20"
   Sur quelle voie se trouve le train? "Voie 20".

9. Is this seat free / taken?
   Est-ce que cette place est libre / occupée?

10. I'm afraid this is my seat.
    C'est ma place.

The Top Ten Airline Travel Phrases

1. When is the next flight to ?
   Quand part le prochain avion pour ?

2. A direct flight
   Un vol direct

3. Where is luggage pick up?
   Où recupère-t-on ses bagages?

4. I'd like a window / an aisle.
   Je voudrais une fenêtre / une allée.

5. Which gate is it at? "Gate 12".
   A quelle porte dois-je aller? "Porte 12".

6. Which way to gate 12?
   Comment puis-je me rendre à la porte 12?

7. My suitcase is lost.
   J'ai perdu ma valise.

8. How long will the flight be delayed?
   L'avion aura un retard de combien?

9. Baggage check.
   Enregistrement des bagages.

10. Where can I confirm the return flight?
    Où dois-je confirmer le vol retour?

The Top Ten Auto Terms

1. Gas / Oil for engine
   L'essence / L'huile pour le moteur

2. Unleaded
   Sans plomb

3. Fill it up, please.
   Le plein, s'il vous plaît.

4. Please check the oil / tires.
   Pouvez-vous vérifier le niveau d'huile / la pression des pneus?

5. My car has broken down.
   Je suis en panne.

6. The car will not start.
   La voiture ne démarre pas.

7. Where is the nearest garage, please?
   Où se trouve le garage le plus proche?

8. I need a tow.
   J'ai besoin d'une dépanneuse.

9. I have had an accident.
   J'ai eu un accident.

10. We need to do a report.
    Nous devons faire un constat.

The Top Ten Hotel Phrases

1. I'd like a single / double room.
   Je voudrais une chambre simple / double.

2. With shower and toilet
   Avec douche et WC

3. With bath and toilet
   Avec bains et WC

4. On the street / on the yard
   Sur la rue / sur cour

5. Do you have any rooms available?
   Est-ce que vous avez des chambres libres?

6. Is breakfast included in the price?
   Est-ce que le petit-déjeuner est inclus dans le prix?

7. At what time is breakfast served?
   A quelle heure est servi le petit déjeuner?

8. Could you please wake me up tomorrow at...?
   Pouvez-vous me réveiller demain à...?

9. I'm sorry, it's too small / too noisy.
   Je regrette, mais elle est trop petite / trop bruyante.

10. Can you show me another room?
    Pouvez-vous me montrer une autre chambre?

The Top Ten Restaurant Phrases

1. I'd like a table for five.
   J'aimerais une table pour cinq personnes.

2. I'd like to reserve a table for tonight.
   J'aimerais réserver une table pour ce soir.

3. The check, please.
   L'addition, s'il vous plaît.

4. Is service included?
   Est-ce que le service est compris?

5. I would like to see the menu.
   Je voudrais voir la carte.

6. I'll have the fixed price menu.
   Je prendrai le menu.

7. Rare / medium / well done.
   Saignant / à point / bien cuit.

8. I am vegetarian.
   Je suis végétarien(ne).

9. I'd like to order.
   J'aimerais commander.

10. Where are the restrooms?
    Où sont les toilettes?

The Top Ten Things on a Menu

1. Starter
   Entrée

2. Main course / Entree
   Plat principal

3. Cheese
   Fromages

4. Dessert
   Dessert

5. Beef
   Boeuf

6. Poultry
   Volaille

7. Fish
   Poisson

8. Seafood
   Crustacés

9. Beverages
   Boissons

10. Ice cream
    Glaces

The Top Ten Wine Phrases

1. Red / white wine
   Vin rouge / blanc

2. I'd like a glass of...
   Je voudrais un verre de...

3. I'd like a bottle of...
   Je voudrais une bouteille de...

4. Champagne
   Champagne

5. The wine list
   La carte des vins

6. Which wine do you suggest?
   Quel vin nous conseillez-vous?

7. A carafe
   Une carafe

8. A half bottle
   Une demi-bouteille

9. A drink before dinner
   Un apéritif

10. A liqueur
    Un digestif / une liqueur

The Top Ten Beverages

1. Coffee black / with milk /with lots of milk
   Café noir / crème / au lait

2. Tea (lemon / sugar)
   Thé (citron / sucre)

3. Hot chocolate
   Chocolat chaud

4. Herbal tea
   Tisane

5. Beer (from the tap)
   Bière (à la pression)

6. Fruit juice
   Jus de fruit

7. Mineral water
   Eau minérale

8. Carbonated / not carbonated
   Gazeuse /Plate

9. Milk
   Lait

10. Tap water
    Eau du robinet

The Internationalist®
International Business, Investment, and Travel

www.internationalist.com

Made in the USA
Las Vegas, NV
22 May 2024